OBJECTS OF
AFFECTION

Also by Sharon Bryan
Salt Air

Wesleyan Poetry

 Wesleyan University Press
Middletown, Connecticut

OBJECTS OF
AFFECTION

Sharon Bryan

Some of the poems in this book appeared originally in *The Anthology of Magazine Verse and Yearbook of American Poetry, The Atlantic Monthly, Georgia Review, The Nation, Ploughshares, Poetry East, Poetry Northwest, Quarterly West, Seattle Review,* and *Western Humanities Review.* "Lunch with Girl Scouts" first appeared in *The Morrow Anthology of Younger American Poets.*

All inquiries and permissions requests should be addressed to the Publisher, Wesleyan University Press, 110 Mt. Vernon Street, Middletown, Connecticut 06457.
Distributed by Harper & Row Publishers, Keystone Industrial Park, Scranton, Pennsylvania 18512.

Library of Congress Cataloging-in-Publication Data
Bryan, Sharon.
    Objects of Affection.
√ (Wesleyan poetry)
    I. Title. II. Series.
PS3552.R877O25   1987   811'.54   85-29512
ISBN 0-8195-2137-X (alk. paper)
ISBN 0-8195-1139-0 (pbk. : alk. paper)

Manufactured in the United States of America

First Edition

Wesleyan Poetry

"Never forgetting him that kept coming constantly so near."

Good friends are beyond worth but not beyond thanking: John, Gloria, Helen, and Margaret Ruff, Gwen Head, Heather McHugh, Ann Lambert, Joanne and Charlie Altieri, Ripley Hugo, Jim and Lois Welch, Maria, Rich, and Richie Sclafani have all fed my head and heart, as well as my face, with their various beautiful soups. Three *are* beyond thanking, but remain as vivid presences in my continuing conversations with them: Richard Blessing, Richard Hugo, and Matthew Hansen.

Contents

III

I

Cheap Seats in the Kingdome

1

There should be switchbacks,
the climb's so steep up the inside
of this man-made rock. No scenery
but the stenciled altimeter numbers:
37. 38. 39. I follow the others
into our row and lean far back
before I can even imagine turning
my eyes to the floor. The players
look like tiddlywinks. There are ten
empty rows, flimsy tin guardrails,
between us and the next people down.
A few fathers and sons sit at the very top,
as if they could pry up the roof
and get out in a hurry if they had to.
I don't want to complain about tickets
I didn't pay for, so I complain
about the man who sold them. You explain
why it wasn't malicious.

2

Then, just as I'm resting my eyes
on the foreground, an angel passes,
right to left, and sits down four
rows in front of us. She has impossibly
beautiful light blond curls, a tan
jacket, jeans, looks about twenty-
five. Her cherubic, straight-haired son
sits happily next to her, her hair
shining over his shoulder. And then,
dear reader, a rat-faced man comes climbing up,
slopping beer from two paper cups
on his shoes, not caring, and hands one
to the angel, who scoots the boy's ass
over, and then her own, but not much.

I could see what they saw in each other,
endless days of saving and being saved,
their thin bones crackling like cellophane.
She never looked at the boy again,
though he bounced and smiled and was
infinitely good. She told him once
to keep it down, but over her shoulder.

3

Fourth quarter an old usher puffs
slowly up in full-dress brown and orange,
hands on his knees every few steps,
scanning all our faces for something.
No one looks guilty, so he crosses
on an empty row, as if that's what he meant
to do all along, just go for a walk,
listen to his lungs fill up, but not
with air, wonder what it would be like
to pitch forward from here, nothing
in his path, to make one last arc
before he lands, white-gloved but
hatless, at the laced feet of the players
and confounded referees.

4

The Sonics are a point behind
with two seconds to go. The in-bounds pass
goes to Thompson, Skywalker, who lifts himself
straight up, pauses, and shoots
from twenty-eight feet out. Three points,
when we only needed two. Our spirits
rise to the roof. Maybe the boy's her
brother, I think. Maybe there's still hope.

Emerson Elementary

Thirty children warm a classroom
with their radiant bodies. Their faces
as they sing are imperfect circles:
eyes, cheeks, each mouth's amazed,

amazing O. *Brightly shone the moon*
that night, though the frost was cru-el . . .
They are so young only a few can read.
The teacher stays just ahead,

showing with her own bright lips
what to say: *when a poor man*
came in sight, gath'ring winter fu-u-el.
No matter how slowly she goes

they stumble over *Wenceslas.* Some giggle,
a few are distraught. They believe entirely
in what they sing, they would give
the poor man their sandwiches

and shoes. Even so, they have not
charity for the bereft and sour-
smelling among them, as if
they thought a bowl must be refilled

only with what it has held.
As if those brimming with mercy
must not spill a drop. The teacher
sees now, almost before the children,

which ones are unlovable. She keeps her hands
to herself, chaste as a lighthouse
rehearsing the possibilities
of shipwreck for motley sailors.

Demolition

Though it's grainy newsprint, the photo
shows each brick and the school's name,
one letter to a block, arched
over the main door. To the sides,
GIRLS and BOYS entrances. But there's more
in the picture, I realize: a crane
stands in one corner, pointing. Between it
and the rectilinear façade, only sticks
and stones. Round as the sun, blurred slightly
by its motion, a wrecking ball lofts
through the haze. Once, a hated teacher here,
monitor of all our errands, refused to let me in
the wrong door, though blood ran from my knee
into my shoe. Still, this is where I learned
the pleasures of moving pen over paper. And,
from an earnest woman in a suit with padded
shoulders, to beware of Mr. Tooth Decay.
I learned enough about my own capacities
for cruelty and loneliness to last a lifetime.
How to hold myself together, and apart.
I can still smell the layers of varnish
darkening initials carved on our desks, taste
chalk dust after someone had been chosen to beat
the erasers. No more need now for literal
bricks than we had for ruled notebooks
when we wrote our arithmetic in the air.

Lunch with Girl Scouts

. . . the spirit intercedes . . . most
eloquently on our behalf . . .

These ten-year-olds all want other names
than their own. I'm Heather, but call me
Laura, says the one who should have played
Lolita in the movie. Her lips are damp
and unbitten. My mother still has a bracelet
she made in camp, with her fantasy name,
Louise, in orange beads. Names can break
our hearts. I've been invited to lunch
with Girl Scouts, to talk to them about
poetry. They're braver than I am, to have gotten
this far. Longing for a uniform,
I spent three weeks as a Brownie. The leader
talked about fly-ups. Soon we would all
fly-up. This meant a plane ride,
or becoming an angel. Either way,
we might die. I quit, with nothing
to show for my torment but a cryptic
pin. The others flew-up—they were
promoted. Once more I'd misfigured
the language I loved. *Round John virgin,*
we sang at Christmas. And I believed
that if I rode my thick Schwinn down
the right alley in springtime, I'd be,
as the song promised, *out at the old*
ball game. There, in the stands, gulping
popcorn, cheering for the Bees. Today
I followed a map into the suburbs,
suddenly shy as I was as a child
but old as the teachers we considered
foreign countries. I begin to take hold
of their various names, but by lunchtime
I haven't said anything useful. My hostess
and I eat quiche, the girls spaghetti.

Pasghetti. They giggle. One says
a two-line poem, and another answers
with four. They're quoting a recent book
they've all read. Each recites
her favorite while the others bounce
on their hands. None of this
is for me. Somehow they've found
a long one they all know and are almost
shouting it in unison. They pull up
their socks without missing a beat,
spill out of the room like marbles.
I stare into my coffee. When was I last
so full of love? So innocent of error?

Lunch at Woolworth's

With lemonade, grilled cheese, and a new book
of poems, I couldn't be happier. The woman
on my right has the special, apple pie
à la mode. Her electric-blue shoes almost
match her dress. "The bottom of my purse
is always good for a couple dollars change,
honey. Let me have a medium Coke."
My packages rest on a shelf under the counter,
the chrome and orange stool is low enough
that my feet are flat on the floor.
I could sit here all day, eavesdropping,
elbows on the counter. The man on my left,
pondering the plastic menu, is too tall
to remind me of the grandfather I adored,
though he has white hair and freckled hands.
The waitress says she's out of hot fudge
but he can have a chocolate sundae,
which she brings in a tulip-shaped dish.
Pleased by his solitary treat, I turn back
to the poet at his wife's bedside,
waiting for her to wake and recover.
After several lines a new voice says,
"No, thanks, I'm just waiting for him."
My imaginary widower has a wife,
a lovely wife, keeping him company
while he spoons up the syrup. Her knees
point toward him and not the counter.
In the book, too, the wife sits up
and smiles. The woman in blue counts the last
of her change. "It isn't much, honey,
but this is for you." The waitress nods
and sweeps it into her hand. We each kiss
our napkins before we get up to go.

Declining *We*

Our late husband and we, says Queen
Victoria in a Monty Python skit.
Her enormous skirts a multitude.
One other person is enough
to make a timid soul royally
inconspicuous. One friend is all
it takes to make me bold. Enchantée
with you, I forget myself, the crooked
seams. *We* is an elm, a gazebo, double-
you, chiaroscuro. *I* is a nail
of noonlight, the squint that will be taken
for surliness in Kodacolor. Though I remember
now, in a French film, Geraldine Chaplin
posing giddily topless for Dominique Sanda.
But that was late afternoon
on a weekend vacation.

    *

We humans, you aliens. You speechless
universe. We who speak
the same language. We who understand
one another's unspoken
cruelties and love. We kin.
We who are allowed to touch,
you who are forbidden. We who think
of death constantly, you who are dead
and so never think of it.
If I could set them all aside,
like a hat, like shoes, like
underwear. But how, in the cold,
would I keep my voice from trembling?
Keep my hands at my sides?
Look steadily at you and never
at my own reflection
winding and unwinding in the lens?

*

Victoria's word became flesh,
a mortal confusion. She was plural
still, after the last corset
was unlatched. If a poem
were a dream, it would mean something
to say I'm all the characters
in it. But to name is not
to be. When I use *we*
I'm speaking wistfully, but out
of turn. My divestiture
is simple: put down a pronoun,
refuse to take it up anew.

I seem to be alone. You too, you too.

Volunteer Work

As the nurses leave after failing to quiet
the baby, each says the same thing, *she's
inconsolable*, holding the word like a stone
that gives a hand something to warm itself around.
Trembling fiercely, she resists our offers of food
and singsong nonsense. Any direction away
from us is north. She may die, but what
can she know of that? For now there's nothing
we would call pain. We're all angry, and vaguely
frightened. She's the first baby ever who wouldn't
take to me, says a woman wearing rhinestone
glasses. Another remembers a wind-up swing, and
finally, out of our hands, Emily sleeps.

Fatigue is a consolation. Whenever we take
consolation, we wanted something else more.
So we hold out, we pass up the bread because
someone might offer us an orange. A new widow
stands in the hall, waiting for her telephone
to stop ringing. We're all deformed or formed
by need—what's the difference? The child unfurls
and stiffens in her mother's absence, the widow's words
begin to warp with her husband's inflections. We knit
our own bones out of what's missing. *Stop crying*
in exchange for what? *Or else* we'll leave you to the ghosts
you prefer to our blooded bodies. What you want
is *out of the question*, like perfume spilled out
of the bottle, so that it stains every breath you take
for a day. For uncountable days. What's your second
choice? Turning cell by cell to stone looking after
your losses? Or letting yourself down into
the desolate present, our arms' lowering horizon?

Out of Mind

1

In a week already frayed by lost time
and lost chances, my cat has vanished,
taking it on herself to make the abstract
unbearably concrete. Even as I try to lift
my voice above the winter rain harrowing
bare ground, even as I mutter into the wind,
poor Harriet, poor Harriet, I know I'm muddying sorrow
with self-pity. A neighbor says he saw her,
but she ran when he opened his door. I imagine
her helpless, hopeless, longing for home. Then I imagine
she fled that pillowed warmth deliberately.
But I can't seem to imagine that she is only
a lost cat, and not the bearer of my various wants
abroad in the world, refusing to come when I call.

2

A Beethoven trio, Ravel. A man next to me asks
how I like the concert so far. I've always found music
healing, I say, and he turns away. I'd explain
if I weren't swathed in migraine, unhealed, unable
to give myself over to what's in front of me.
My cat is still missing in the year's worst storm,
and I am beyond the reach of reason and good manners,
trying to wish her home. Ridiculous, I chide, even
as I leave early. The rain has finally thinned
to mist. I know where to look tonight, tomorrow,
the day after. I can't imagine an end to looking.
But when I park and go inside to change my shoes,
Harriet is curled on the couch, licking herself dry.
A note from my neighbor says he coaxed her inside
with food. She yawns as if she'd never been gone,
and I can no more summon her absence
than I could her presence. We are each returned
to our nonchalant, warm-blooded bodies, and will sleep
tonight deep inside them, as if we had traveled
unspeakable distances to restore our separate spirits.

Night Light

1

Middle of the night, linoleum
so cold it made my feet ache.
Between the bathroom's two
mirrors, my great-grandmother
was brushing her hair. I'd never
seen it unpinned before. The red
she'd been notorious for
flashed through gray, her mouth
turned even further down
than usual. Neither of us spoke.
Back in bed I watched my lamp,
a forest fire painted on celluloid,
revolve on the dresser. Precise
little flames trilled in the black
branches, orange smoke rose to the brim.

2

An odd comfort for a child.
I wonder what I'd make of it
now, its immortal danger and gaudy
colors. The memory isn't enough.
Or it's too much. I want the lamp
so I can stop thinking of it,
and sleep. As for my grandmother,
she takes care of herself. Her arm
rises and falls, her hair crackles.
She is vanishing into both mirrors,
front and back, as vividly as ever.
Her nightgown sways, her face shines
unshaded. I never loved her in the flesh.

Cinéma Vérité

You have to know the title
for this movie to mean
anything: Joe DiMaggio Hitting
a Home Run in Yankee Stadium.
A small shape stutters
in one corner, then travels
distinct base paths in two
seconds. The film is soundless,
jumpy, pale green and yellow.
It's an heirloom—worthless
except as we gather around it
saying its name. Fingerprints
on the screen smudge the infield,
the projector rattles *continuo*
through our several voices. History
is incidental—what connects us
in the flickering light is love
of counterpoint, of the terrible
pauses between known and
answering known. Joe, almost
washed away by light,
is a relief. Most of the films
open with a series of dark
frames, my grandfather's
specialty. We claim to forget
what's coming. Arteries
of lightning at dusk
somewhere in Nebraska. The full
moon from a moving train.
The Rockettes' flashing thighs
at Radio City Music Hall.
Then the bright blank screen
poised against our ingenuity
until one of us, stumbling
and apologizing, finds the lamp.

We avert our eyes. Our flesh
is only flesh, not some
aspect of light. We're hungry
enough to eat cold roast
at midnight, so sleepy we yawn
with our mouths full, talk
of nothing but tomorrow's weather.

Das Boot

1

A submarine is a kind of life-
support system, an iron lung
for those endangered and out
of their element. No visitors,
no natural light, little to do
but shit and piss and joke about sex
where everyone can hear. When the dials
head into the red, the only sounds
are tentative breaths, then the irregular
thuck of popping rivets. Each man must want
more than anything, when the lung
begins to fail, to put on two dry shoes,
stroll on steady land-legs out of there.

2

WW II. The German crewmen
reveal themselves under pressure,
inside the hull's resonant, taut walls.
Over and over, with improvised tools,
they save their own lives. It's surfacing
they can't survive: out of nowhere,
enemy planes. Strafing, shells. In minutes
everyone's dead except the reporter
over whose shoulder we've been watching
the innocent blonds and redheads,
the experienced captain. Gloves float by,
a loose shoe. Iridescent waters
open a hundred tender letters home.

3

A patient who can't live outside
intensive care is as fragile
an illusion as a fictional
character, made vivid by confinement

and irreducible gesture—drawled
vowels, mock scowl, a subterranean
laugh. The character does most
of the work, but avid readers
help keep things going when X is dozing
or indisposed, making a life
out of intermittent words. No wonder
they begin to see X on the real street,
hurrying around a corner in the rain.

4

Savor is a deeper pleasure
than suspense. The second time through
a character's life, the details
are poignant because an uncertain
future no longer pulls them
out of shape. Each one is full
of itself as the ripe fruit offered
the heroic submariners
at a glittering banquet before
their last mission. It's the food
they've dreamed of, but it can't sustain them.
They hurry back to the dim ship,
run at periscope depth through flaming waves
for the straits of Scylla and Charybdis.

5

When someone ill is *holding his own*,
his belly's still wrapped around his life,
he can let his breath go
and call it back, make a fist, refract
our assumptions about him. We're as glad
to see him as if we had surfaced
mid-ocean to discover a friend
crossing our bow. We lean into

the wind to keep our feet. Later,
when we say he's *failing badly*,
we mean he's stopped resisting us,
he's lost his specific gravity.
We'll tell each other he's dead,
close over him, be his undoing.

Hollywood's *Titanic*

Disaster films are an hour and a half
of foreplay, then when death finally comes
the camera pans discreetly
to the women and children arrayed
at a safe distance in lifeboats,
wringing their gloves. On the steep deck,
a band was leading the men in hymns
when a final explosion shook
the camera so the faces blurred,
but not before I had seen the eyes widen
—to take in what? Who died
by fire and who by water? How many
took their instruments with them?
Did some try to run, even
under water? What makes so many
say *I'm dead* and not *I'm dying*,
as if the voice had turned back
to hurry the dawdling body?
Though the sea's almost calm
as glass, even a breath dissolves
the images that rise to the surface,
drowns the ragged chorus of last words.

Hopper's *Early Sunday Morning*

We look straight on
at the shops—barber,
unmarked others, the curtained,
blinded windows of the second-
floor apartments implying
sleepers and dreamers.
The fire hydrant's elegant
thin shadow exactly
parallels the curb,
an arrow pointing west
like the heads of proper
dead. The sun must be
just up the road,
the town must have been
laid out like Stonehenge
to map the light's
coming and going. Today
the sun will pass un-
hurriedly along the street
kept clean all year,
but for now each doorway's
dark with possibility.

Madonnas in the Fogg

Paintings deck the halls
chronologically. The first wall
is all red-and-gold divinity,
attenuated figures afloat

under helmet-like haloes.
Mary's half-moon face turns
our attention to her son's
wise eyes and slender,

upraised fingers. Wait. Not
that he is about to speak,
for who would imagine tongues
in these perfect heads? Just

wait, until the body's local
weather no longer clouds
your vision, nothing stands
between you and pure idea

except its bright colors
and seductively modeled forms.
But today I'm too cold
to stand still, even for en-

lightenment, so I keep walking
past all the theology, around
the corner to the Baroque. And stop,
still, at Gentileschi's *Madonna*

with the Sleeping Christ Child. Mother
and son, flesh and blood, the weight
of his left foot in her
right hand. He is mortally

asleep, unclothed, his pale skin
tinged rose, like the apricot
he holds in one hand. Mary lifts
her scarf, as if to shield him

from any breeze. The moment ripens
unbearably, makes me long to be held
by the things of this world. A lifetime
of looking won't wake the painted child.

Pictures of Nothing

1

Don't think of pigs. Or socks,
or telephone poles. This was a joke,
like punching someone on the arm.
A dare, a little lesson in the impossible.

So when we all crouched under our desks
listening to the teacher's instructions,
I knew the first thing I'd do if a bomb fell
would be to look at the light

before it washed over me. Yet now
the adult I am flinched back
from a painting, its yellow-and-white blaze
uncontained by the ornate frame. *Turner,*

said the calm brass placard, while
the waves rose and broke. I wept
and shook my head. *I didn't know,*
I didn't know. As if in the present

I did know something, though I stood there
dumb and blind. Not the light
that illuminates, but the light
that obliterates. The mind cleared by a stone

hurled into its small pond. Nothing left
to contemplate but this violent abstraction.
Except my progress seems to be
from error to error. This is Venice,

with the sun overhead. The green-and-gold
vortex across the room is *Interior*
at Petworth. The titles are half
the story. I should have saved my tears

for what the paint so faithfully renders:
every shimmering veil that divides us
from the world we long to hold. And white
the sum of all the world's refusals.

 2

Mummies are a kind of pearl
with the body as seed, the layers
of gauze blurring and evoking

their occasion, generalizing
the particular. More *aide-mémoire*
than *memento mori*. So how is it

we came to swaddle the dead
in stone? Some heroes in the crypt
at St. Paul's rest in granite, in marble,

in porphyry boxes, raised or reduced
to geometry, to names and dates. More
lie under the floor—Christopher Wren,

for one, as a kind of signature
to his own greatest work, which aspires
less to heaven than to history. No

landscape intrudes, none of these dead
will escape by disguising themselves
as grass. Even the pineapples

carved on the west tower were chosen
for their perfect form, not their
succulence. This is no place for hunger,

for thirst, for sorrow. Yet someone
has brought a small bouquet—a rose,
two carnations, some daisies, still wrapped

in green tissue—and laid it across
one stone: J. M. W. Turner, 1775–1851.
After all the disembodied praise,

it's an accident of affection,
a wound at the heart of things,
that brings me to my knees.

3

And again to tears. But what
does all this weeping have to do
with art? It's a way of saying
thank you for the hand that cast me

out of myself, the radiant
energy, the eye that didn't blink
at a world in flames; the sublime vapor;
the residue of ash; its given names.

The End of Rose's Streak

It's the sports record least likely to be broken:
Joe DiMaggio hit safely in 56 games in a row.
How I hated finding out, at eight, what it meant
to hit safely. He *did* hit it, I'd whine, squinting
at the snowy Magnavox. Yes, but the fielder
caught it, said my patient grandmother. The worst news
was that the catcher signaled the pitcher, secretly,
what to throw, runners looked to their coaches,
the manager managed it all. They're not taking
any chances, the announcer would rumble, as the pitcher
left, head down, for the showers. But chances
were what I wanted. And now there's a chance Pete Rose
might break Joe's record. Each day a new chapter,
Dickens serialized on the sports page. He keeps us going—
sometimes it's the ninth inning before he gets a hit.
Thirty games, forty. He waves to each player he passes,
tips his hat. Two more games, he tells reporters,
and he's going after Sidney Stonestreet. Who?
He pauses, grins: I made him up. He got fifty.
No way I can get from here to Joe without someone
in between. But it never happens. Comes a game
when Rose grounds out, flies out, strikes out. Like that
he's done—was done the day before at 44,
tied with Wee Willie Keeler. Rather than weep
in public, he berates the pitcher for throwing
as if it were the World Series. He is finally graceless,
bitter, unheroic. Hitting is child's play. Hitting
safely is artifice, meaning only some of the connections
count. Tomorrow, when Pete lifts his bat, he will not
be part of any story. Pitches will rise out of the dark
like moths, whether he swings frantically or de-
liberately. Too many chances, not too few. And I will unfold
the morning paper, its grimy blizzard of facts, my hopes
unpinned, adrift, looking for something to settle on
that will make them visible but not unbearably so.

Home

Puny poems. The end is always
in sight, this page or the next,
no child begs for one more stanza,
no besotted reader postpones
finishing until tomorrow—that sweet
delay in which time and the characters
pause. Believing Pnin had broken
a glass dish, his only token of love
received, I put down Nabokov's novel
to keep from breaking Pnin's heart, and mine,
but N. had seen to that, the dish
was whole. A good novel takes us in
as thoroughly as if we were homeless
waifs, gives us the run of the place,
few burdensome chores. So fingering
the final pages there's a certain
desperation at the loneliness
to follow. We can come back, of course,
but later, informed by loss and pending loss.

II Reading Proust

Where Is Marcel's Father?

Supervising the weather. Then forecast
on the stairway by his candle's
wavering shadow. *I'm done for,*
thinks Marcel, accidentally correct
before his father's offhand kindness:
he gives the boy the boy's beloved
mother. What ineluctable
fictional need kept a generous man
offstage for the next three thousand
pages? Not just absent but impossible
to imagine, ungathered, disbanded,
except for a brief appearance
at the grandmother's deathbed? Realism
isn't the issue. If the father is half
a metaphor, what's the other term?
Marcel, perhaps, forever missing
as husband, father; the first-person
narrator inventing himself
out of mirrors and a moustache;
the weather staining every blessèd page.

Mother Tongue

She said not a single word to me, and indeed I used to
go days on end without being spoken to for far more
venial offenses than this . . .

Ah, Marcel, *cher enfant,*
why only half a sentence
for the greatest pain?
What did your loving mother

have in mind? Perhaps she tucked
the words meant for you into other
conversations, so that her babble
thickened the air more than usual,

like the scents of your favorite dinner
being simmered for company.
Perhaps you kept quiet all day
not to miss a precious syllable.

Or tried innocent questions
hoping to trip her up. There's so much
I'd like to ask you. Both of you—
the fictional child, the author

who lived and died. For *days on end:*
in those words you seem joined
as by an arrow at the breastbone.
Your mother's exquisite cruelty

provokes me to tears, so here I am
trying to repair her silence,
to fill your delicate ears
with the sound of your name.

Marcel, Marcel. What vanity
to pretend you can hear me.
And while I seem to speak to you,
what living hearts go unattended?

Mme. P. to Her Dead Mother

He was a beautiful boy,
maman, but so harsh—
and perverse as the wind.
Who could guess when he wanted lies
and when the truth? Today
he announced it's my fault
he's decided to marry. I am never
clever enough. What a charming girl,
I should have said, why don't you see
more of her? Too late. Now how long
can I hold my breath? I wear
your clothes and read your books,
still I don't know how to love him
as well as you did. I heard him weeping
in the night, and when I went in
he mistook me for you. For a moment,
I'm sure, there was a chance
somehow to change our lives. But I spoke,
the room became familiar,
everything was lost.

Swann in Love

Bunches of cattleyas! That's what Odette
is holding. She's strewn with them,
bedecked, festooned. The crucial ones
riffle their mauve petals in the valley
of her bosom. Odette consents that Swann
should rearrange what the jarring carriage
has unsettled. Just last week my own cattleya
bloomed for the first time in four years,
a single white blossom, fleshy
and ethereal, stained yellow at the throat.
I kept quiet as its bud swelled, for fear
it would drop unopened. I walk by it slowly,
so I won't make a draft. Queen and snake,
Cleopatra and her asp fused in one flower
that seems to hold itself deliberately still
in my study window. Odette and Swann
embrace with the zeal of relief. He failed
to find her, after an evening's search,
in another man's arms. She, fresh
from another man's arms, saves herself
by giving herself to Swann. How could anyone
who would heap orchids in her hair
distinguish manners from passion? Surely everything
she touched was room temperature. Except
Swann, perhaps, who invents language
out of his own shyness and terror.
Doing a cattleya comes to mean, for these two,
making love. Each day my tethered flower
is a little tamer, more itself. I turn it
away from the sun toward the room,
from getting to spending. I hoped for a bloom,
but I didn't intend it. Out of such
accidents of heat and light and longing,

we make love. Out of looking and looking
away. So little of all that exists
ever shows itself. Still it's infinitely more
than we can take in. To admit the shining world,
we empty ourselves into love.

The Fugitive

Now I see why, for all its charm,
The Sweet Cheat Gone was a diminished
title. The fault lies not with Albertine
but in our inability to follow,
to find in the daytime the piazza
discovered at night, to know living
from dead, male from female, sorrow
from the palms of our hands. Cathedrals
flicker as if they were made of water
and light, and they are, for this
is Venice. Gilberte's signature, misread
by the telegrapher, restores Albertine
briefly to an indifferent
present. We are sure we will stay;
at the last minute we catch the train.

We could mistake *fleeting* for *fleeing*,
and imagine the world hurries away
from us. If it eludes us, if we cannot
quite put our finger on it, still
we have it in translation, we feel
the weight of our own limbs, of the cities
around us. The book is heavy
in my lap. When I look up from it
I see late afternoon sky framed
by the triptych of living-room windows,
making visible what they cannot contain.

View of Delft

1

When Borges was nearly blind,
his favorite ties were yellow,
the only color he could see.
When Bergotte is dying, sprawled
like a hopeless lover
opposite the Vermeer, he is held
by a small patch of yellow
glittering on a stone wall.
Photographers call these circles of light
"points of confusion," but on canvas,
in deliberate oil, one's enough
to show a man his heart turning
its pockets out. For that long his life
dwarfs any daubed city, as if a cinder
obscured his vision, but already
it's too late to rectify things
by weeping. Which is the sun,
the life or the work, and which
the mottled, implacable moon?

2

After a death so conclusive,
what's Bergotte doing up and around
five hundred pages later, a regular
visitor to Gilberte and St. Loup?
Perhaps that scene was to be carried
whole, like a painting,
to a quieter wall. For now
it's used for irony: Albertine
lies that she was with Bergotte.
The narrator assumes, reflexively,
the newspaper has mistaken
the death date. We're with Albertine
in this, impatient with Marcel's will

to be duped. None of us has the power
to bring him out of his trance.
Maybe this seemed too small a use
of death—one more straw
on the blaze of lies, one more shimmer
in the overheated air.

3

Cottard's death is good
for a feeble joke, or a final
dignity in the Great War.
If Oriane dies, Gilberte will marry
the Duc. These are the author's musings,
not the narrator's
hallucinations. Questions
of shape and texture rather than
delirious need. Then Proust himself
lay cool and mute amid the twining
marginalia, and characters without
a single vanishing point
stood forever out of focus. Raveled
ends, flapping sheets waiting to be filled
and lifted whole, all of us waiting
for them to carry us aloft
where we can see earth in thin air.

The Life

The biographer implies
the work of art is a translation
of the life: Here
in the flesh
is the original of Swann.
Mama, Grandmama,
the irrepressible steeple.
The Duchesse de Guermantes
was pieced from four
cruelly elegant people.
Proust's brother
must have been poetry
if poetry is what can't be
translated. No seam
or shadow of his absence,
but a whole world
without him, turning to
and from the sun,
and he is not
down any of the streets
gathered at the horizon,
nor in any man's or woman's
arms, nor on the lips
of any sleeper. Some slight
trepidation in the heavens
perturbs the astronomers,
but Robert—Robert is neither
here nor there.

III

But love is only one of many passions. . . .
Samuel Johnson

Breaking and Entering

No big deal, locking ourselves
out of the house your first
night back. But that quickly
we were trapped in allegory,
Despair totting up a locksmith's
overtime, Hope checking for loose
latches. Thank God for the window
we should have fixed months ago.
You pried the screen off, almost
Disappointed. I was un-
flaggingly Jaunty climbing in.
For all that, it was a lovely moment,
knocking the pepper mill into the cat
food, trying to keep my knees
out of the bacon grease. I know,
I can't have it both ways. Did this
crime mean anything or not?
I think we were both passionately
afraid, but even small emergencies
are a chance to be brave. Our lives
are no mystery: we could pawn
the loaded gun instead of firing it.
We broke, we entered. May that be
enough violence to hold us fast.

If Nobody Dies It's a Comedy,

not a tragedy. If the same
is true of life, none of us
gets more than one tragic
starring role. The grieving family

should not take home the roses.
You and I should not mistake
our squabbles for greater stuff.
Neither of us will die of parting

or of staying, though we weep
and rage and hug our pain
to our chests like a beloved
only child. We both believe

and disbelieve in loss, as when
a mother tells the son she hasn't
seen in twenty years she always knew
he'd come back. Doesn't that mean

she failed to wring her heart dry?
Apparently even the longest arcs
of ordinary sadness can be redeemed
by a happy ending, one that un-

perplexes. Then what of the years
the violin was in the pawnshop?
The lost son living around the corner
from the listless mother? Time passed,

say the stories, as if each day were not
covered with its own particular lint.
Time passed, as water might, under
a trout that hesitates in the air

it's leapt to. Comedies end here,
in unrefracted light falling
on bare faces, each character nodding
with knowledge and forgetfulness.

In life, the stream rethreads
the trout; my heart regathers
each loss without missing a beat;
I remember too much to be wise.

What I Want

I don't see any wolves at first,
they're so limply asleep
in the dry grass. Then one lifts

its head, teeters to its feet,
turns its snout in our direction
for a long minute before the strings

let go and he refolds himself
to sleep. Now I know what to look for,
I count six bags of bones

you've come to the zoo to say
good-bye to. I've come to say good-bye
to you, and I want the wolves you love

to rise and press their noses to the fence.
As if they could absolve me
of anything. They are oblivious

to the weight of what I want,
what you want. You carry yourself
as if you might break, while I praise

the reticulate giraffe
because it has no lessons to teach us.
Not one beautiful animal in here

wants to hold us, except as food.
Because I don't know what to say to you,
I've never been so tired of words.

And so tired of my body, which will not
hold you any more than the wolves
will come forward to ease your going.

Bad News

A friend is ill, a cousin dead.
I know what to say when I call
and your voice, like matchlight,
summons your face. I almost know,
from your silences, what not to say.

This is safe ground, the king's X
of childhood games, charmed circle,
crossed fingers, time out. The tenuous
terms of estrangement. Wires thin
as human hair suspend the universe

we were once the center of. I can't
remember if light travels forever
with nothing to stop it, or if
the dark drinks it as the earth does
a river. I pause mid-sentence.

Now even loss is something
we no longer have in common.
You say you hope next time the news
will be better. I stand on one foot—
because, like the bird in the joke,

I'd fall down if I didn't.
In the future no news will be
good enough, the road we've abandoned
a faint derangement of the landscape,
visible only from the air.

The Unknown

This or that. Find the predicate.
Everything else is the subject.
Who are you in love with
now? Not-X. It's the principle
of exclusion. Not-X is taller,

softer, kinder, all of these
inevitably. Defined by *er*—and
est, ungrammatically. As the night
the night, X is the dreaded double
negative, not-not. Small potatoes

compared to the rest of the
unparalleled universe. Unspud
stars, unspud hands to hold. Es-
pecially unspud ears to bend
with the sad little songs we know

by unrelenting heart. Enough
to keep us distrait undoing,
undoing. It's midnight.
The victims are about to back into
the gloved hands of the killers.

Even undeceived we scream
and wake up, scream and wake.
The dream of experience is about
to be submerged by the dream
of innocence, new potatoes.

Alone at the Movies

The title is *Fanny and Alexander*,
but by intermission the girl hasn't
done much but shine her face
at her older brother and the women
of the house: nannies, aunties, cooks,
her golden mother. She looks on unfazed
at her father's death, her brother's
cowering, his brave humiliations. Why not
leave out a part so small? She is his
measure, his annotator, the anticipated
ear into which he'll rehearse
the story of his life—his breath
taking shape in the unheated bedroom
while a magic-lantern horseman gallops
across the bare wall. Twenty-year-olds
in front of me groan at the silliness
of an old man's movie, but at forty
my sympathies are undivided. An entire
argument—a point of view—unfolds
as I stand in the dark, glasses
in hand. But it all depends on one
particular listener, one other's
memory. The distance between two eyes
revises what each reports, embodies
the phantom. Sometimes now everything
seems equally far away: stairs;
the sidewalk; home. Dreams lost
to waking; days undone by sleep.

Abiding Love

1

I know all that's wrong with coveting
your neighbor's life, but I want the one
I've invented for this couple in front of me
in line at the license bureau. I can see
the pulse in his temple, the faint down
along her jaw. But I can't understand
their constant murmurings, so practiced
they are at keeping in and keeping out.
She's 70 and beautiful, he's matter-of-
factly rapt. They never quite touch,
though they incline themselves to receive
whatever's given. I study the driver's
handbook, memorizing numbers I'll forget
tomorrow. Before she steps away
for the official photograph, she reties
the bow at her throat. Her husband's shoes
are freshly shined, his neck pink
from the barber's clippers. When his wife
comes shyly back he lifts his arms,
asking her to dance. My own rise up in reply.

2

I'm not pleased to be so angry, reading
Williams' "Asphodel," nor to have taken so long
to get angry. Those hypnotic looping lines
must have distracted Flossie, too. Though I'm confusing
the life with the work. And it's not in the poem
that Williams says, of an audience of en-
thralled young women: *they were adorable,*
I could have raped them all. Then the talk
is of gardens, of Helen, of the siren seas.
Scheherazade didn't talk any faster or more
dissuasively. But after all the scarves
and sleight of hand, the question of forgiveness
turns out to be rhetorical. The speaker passes
unscathed from the damned to the saved,
from frog to prince without the kiss. An extra
line of white space marks the act itself. So much
for a woman's pain and grace. If *nothing is impossible*
for the imagination, why didn't her husband just imagine
the intimate aromas of other women's bodies?

3

Persephone was picking asphodel
just before her violent coronation.
Ovid says she wept most for the scattered
flowers; later carpeted her dim living room
with their pale stars. Half the year
in thrall to her sullen husband,
half to her mother—doted on
coming and going, her goodness a pool
for rinsing sin and sorrow. Her knees
remember the grass, and her heart
its greed: she wanted the unfamiliar
flowers, next thing she knew she was queen
of hell. *Non sequitur?* Her fault? She almost
dreads the spring, which blinds her each year
with hope. Like any bride, she believed
she could save her husband from himself.
He too believed that. *Folie à deux.*

4

Narcissus: *I'll die before I give you power over me.*
Echo: *I give you power over me.*

In the days before his distillation,
Narcissus studied in vain for something
to love in the water's account of his face.
Saw that the women who claimed to love him
must be lying, so was filled with contempt
for them too. May have been haunted
by his beginnings: his mother almost drowned
in a brook as she was raped by his father.
No wonder the man's first sight of himself
scorched his eyes. No wonder he ran
from the sound of his own words
on Echo's lips. No wonder he died of thirst.
Even then his untouchable double looked up
from the sinuous river of hell.

Narcissus is a kind of asphodel.

Echo, who had thought her words
safely couched in his, still glows
with shame. No one to please, no one
to hide behind. So deep the habit
of answering, she doesn't know where
to begin. She loved. But the body that burned
with love cools in the forest's
filtered days. Dissolves, rises. What a relief
to be free of memory in the flesh. No hands
full of anger, no pockets of pain. Only knots
of air, tying and untying themselves.
The realm of perfect love and perfect
loneliness. Nothing attaches her to earth
but the imperfect words she gathers
from the lips of the living.

5

Past and present are so intertwined,
you can't abandon one without losing your grip
on the other. Says a pompous psychiatrist
of the amnesiac hero in an early Ross MacDonald.
The hero has help, a woman who loves him
desperately. It's almost slapstick, the way
they bump into the facts of his life.
Someone murdered his wife. Simple, you say,
and the other woman does have a secret.
Until memory begins to beat its way
into view, like a bat down from the attic,
and he discovers himself stepping back,
knife in hand, from his wife's ruined body.
The woman watching him now—he'd called
for her help, then forgotten all of it.
He's ashamed of the skin that makes him
visible. Yet when he looks into his cupped hands,
he sees he needs not justice but mercy. The woman
says she's not afraid of him. *Everything she's done,*
she wanted to. But she is afraid of the secret
balanced between them like an awkward sofa
as they climb the stairs; she imagines its violent
slide. *To him she says more cheerful things.*

6

One more. Psyche fell in love with Eros
in the dark, with the stories he told her
and those she told herself as he slept.
She had never been happier or more afraid:
each night his steadfast longing, each night
his steadfast refusal to show himself.
Don't look. It was one of those silly tests
a lover is bound to fail. When Psyche lit the candle,
she saw a man already in flight. What could she do,
if she loved him, but follow? She went
from one impossible task to the next, until
she almost forgot what she had come for.
Eros seemed two men, and she wondered which
she wanted. Which she would find. Most versions
give the reunion such short shrift, it can't
have been the point. Psyche's only secret
was that she had no desire to be immortal,
but had walked around the world to heal
her double vision, to forget either half
of what she had seen. The moral was
that she should have trusted him, said Eros,
but he was the one with something to hide.

7

Just one more.
Isak Dinesen tells of telling her lover stories
as they sailed under the stars of long African nights
kneeling on her oriental rugs. She spoke less
to save her life than to postpone daylight's
faded colors. And the tales were so compelling
years later, when she sat down to write
Out of Africa, that she could not stop inventing:
Denys had no home but hers; he was killed
flying back to their farm. As if his house
south of hers were immaterial, and the ring
returned at their parting not heavy
in her pocket. But those things had happened
to Karen Blixen, not Isak, *the one who laughs,*
the one whose words imply a beloved listener.

8

A peeling white arch announces the World's
Longest Beach. The tide's out, leaving a film
that doubles the view. The sand seems to open
onto stacked clouds and patches of blue.
But nothing falls through. At the waterline,
kittywakes chase each wave back out to sea.
Their little stick legs seem to have been drawn
with crayon, and blur when the birds run—
they *will not* fly. But a startled gull rises
and its twin sinks into the counterfeit sky
below. It's a child's question: where does it go?
And the woman who so resembles me, her watery
sun, her world about to be undone? Present, past.
Abide, abode. Open the doors and let them in.

ABOUT THE AUTHOR

Sharon Bryan's first book of poetry, *Salt Air* (Wesleyan New Poets, 1983) won a Governor's Citation from the Washington State Library in 1985. Other awards have included first prize from the Academy of American Poets, University of Iowa (1976), the "Discovery" / *The Nation* award (1977) and a National Endowment for the Arts award. She has received degrees from the University of Utah (B.A. 1965), Cornell University (M.A. 1969), and The University of Iowa (M.F.A. 1977). She is associate professor of English at Memphis State University and editor of the *Memphis State Review*.

ABOUT THE BOOK

Objects of Affection was composed in Weiss type by G&S Typesetters of Austin, Texas, printed on 60-pound Glatfelter B-31 paper by McNaughton & Gunn Lithographers of Saline, Michigan, and bound by John Dekker and Sons of Grand Rapids, Michigan. The design is by Joyce Kachergis Book Design and Production of Bynum, North Carolina.

Wesleyan University Press, 1987